My name is ____.

My birthday is on ________________________________.

My favourite hobbies are ___________________________

____

____

This is a picture of me.

Trace over

cl cl cl cl cl cl

Copy

cl

Make cl words.

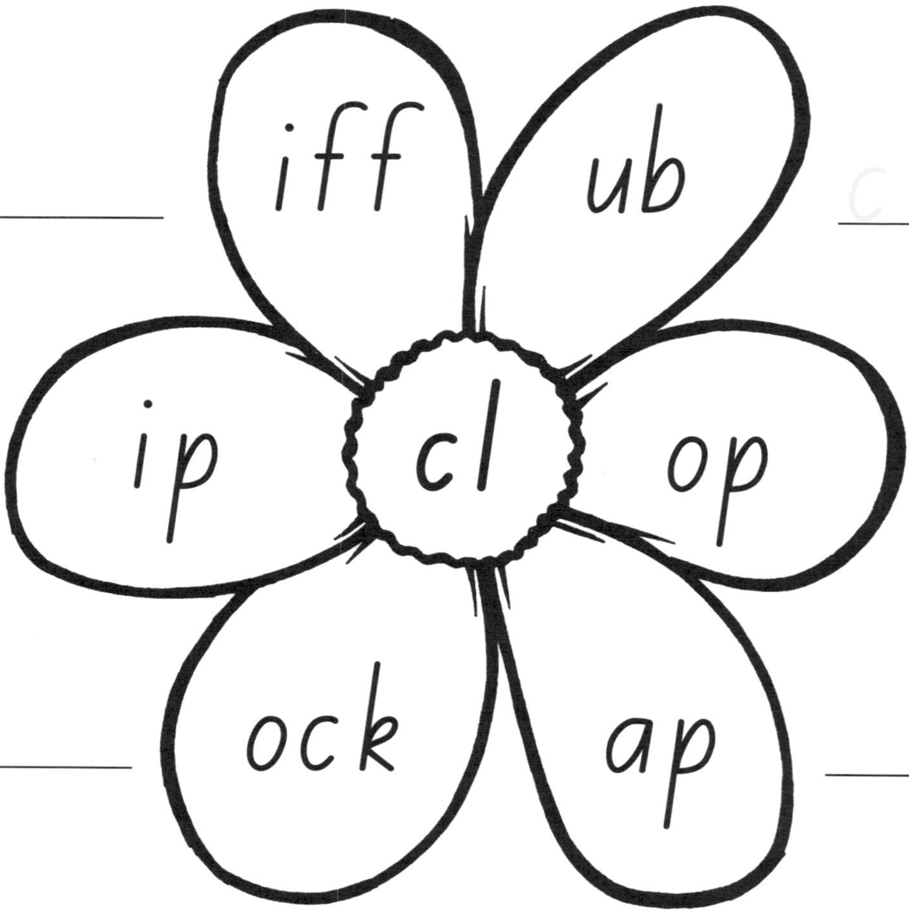

club

Write cl words in the shapes.

cl

fl

Trace over

fl fl fl fl fl fl

Copy

fl

Trace over the fl words in red. Hint! There are three fl words.

f	l	i	p	a	l
l	k	f	l	o	p
i	f	l	a	g	k

Trace over the correct fl word.

The (flag, flip) is on the flagpole.

Trace over

bl bl bl bl bl

Copy

bl ______________________________

Add bl and trace over the word endings.

__ __ast

__ __ack

__ __iss

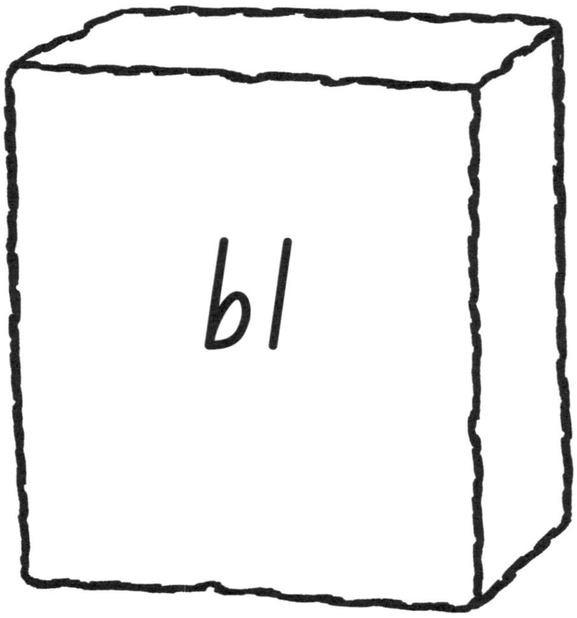

__ __ock

__ __ink

__ __ob

Write the same bl word twice to finish the sentence.

Colour the __ __ __ __ __ bird

__ __ __ __ __.

bl

sl

Trace over

sl sl sl sl sl sl

Copy

sl

Trace over the sounds and write the new word.

sl + ug = ____________

sl + op = ____________

sl + ap = ____________

sl + ip = ____________

Finish the sentence.

In the summer, we have to

sl__ __, sl__ __, sl__ __!

Trace over

gl gl gl gl gl

Copy

gl

Add gl and trace over the word endings.

__ __um

__ __ad

__ __ass

__ __oss

Trace over the correct gl word.

1. I feel (glat, glad) when you hug me.

2. Can I have a (glass, gless) of water?

gl

st

Trace over

st st st st st st

Copy

st ______________________

Make st words.

op stop ______________________

ep ______________________

uck ______________________

ill ______________________

Trace over the sounds and add st. Draw pictures.

ne__ __	lo__ __	re__ __

Trace over

sc sc sc sc sc sc

Copy

sc

Trace over the sc words in red. Hint! There are four sc words.

t	S	s	c	o	o	p
b	s	c	a	r	f	d
s	c	o	o	t	e	r
m	s	y	o	t	t	g

Draw a girl on a scooter wearing a scarf.

SC

sk

Trace over

sk sk sk sk sk

Copy

sk

Trace over the sounds and write the new words.

sk + ip = ______

sk + id = ______

sk + in = ______

sk + ull = ______

Write sk words in the shapes.

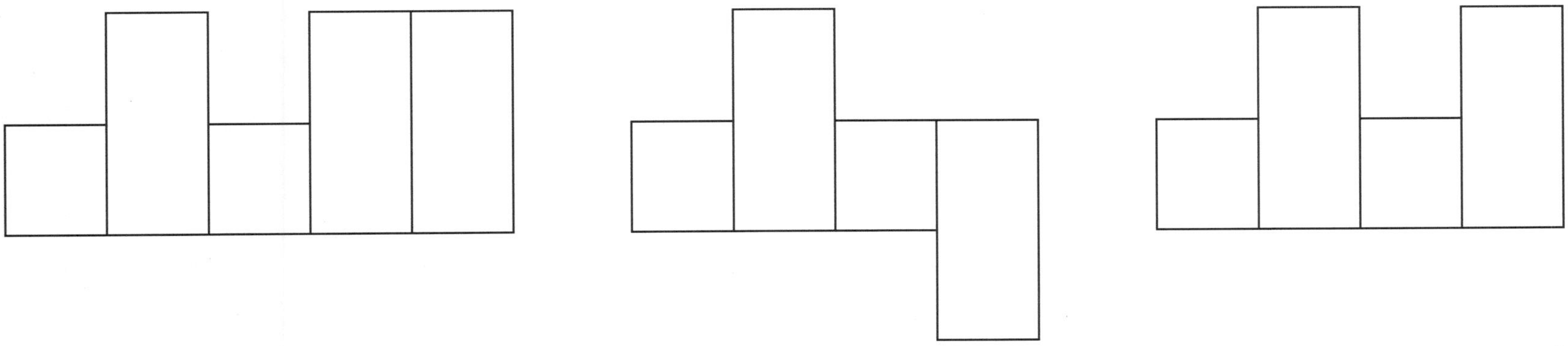

Trace over

sm sm sm sm sm

Copy

sm ______________________________

Make *sm* **words.**

smart __________ __________ __________

__________ __________ __________

Write *sm* **words to finish the sentences.**

1. I can _ _ _ _ _

   the pretty flowers.

2. We have to stop _ _ _ _ _!

sm

sn

Trace over

sn sn sn sn sn

Copy

sn

Add sn and trace over the word endings.

___ ___ug

___ ___ap

___ ___ag

___ ___iff

___ ___ob

___ ___ip

Finish the puzzle with sn words.

	s		
	n		g
			p

Trace over

sp sp sp sp sp sp

Copy

sp

Trace over the sp words in red. Hint! There are five sp words.

s	p	i	d	e	r
s	p	o	r	t	s
p	p	e	d	x	p
i	o	e	l	e	o
n	a	c	y	l	t

What am I?

I have 8 legs and 8 eyes. I spin a web.

___ ___ ___ ___ ___ ___

sp

sw

Trace over

sw sw sw sw sw

Copy

sw

Trace over the sounds and write the new sw words.

sw + im = ______________

sw + ing = ______________

sw + ell = ______________

sw + eet = ______________

Write sw words to match the pictures.

__ __ __ __   __ __ __ __ __

Trace over

br br br br br

Copy

br

Add *br* and trace over the word endings.

__ __ing

__ __ick

__ __im

__ __ush

__ __anch

Finish the puzzle with *br* words.

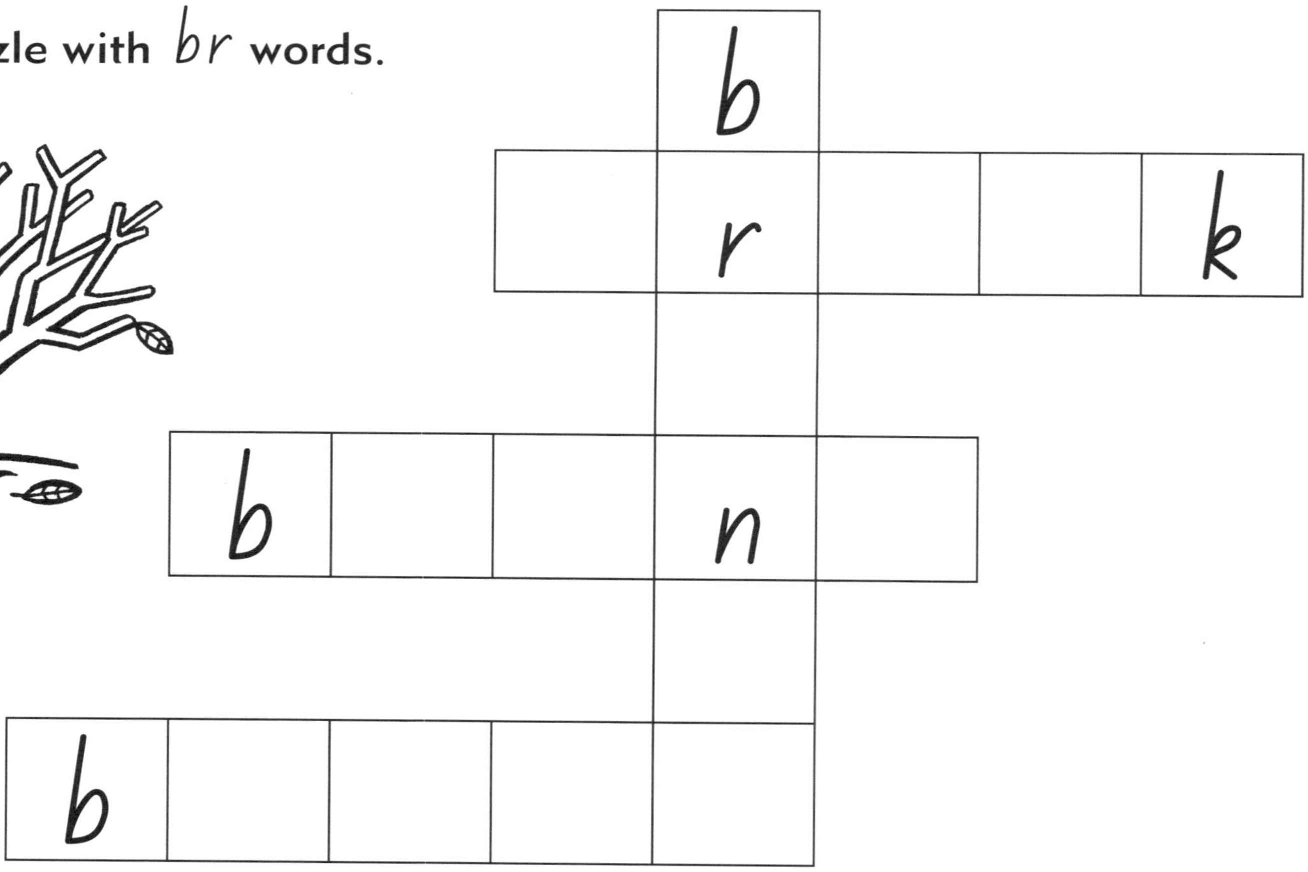

br

cr

Trace over

cr cr cr cr cr cr

Copy

cr

Trace over the cr words.

crisp

creek

crab

cross

crop

cramp

crash

Trace over the correct cr word.

1. I like to swim in the (creer, creek).

2. I saw a big (crab, crad) in a rock pool.

Trace over

dr dr dr dr dr dr

Copy

dr ____________________

Add dr and trace over the word endings.

__ __ ag

__ __ ip

__ __ ank

__ __ ess

__ __ ink

__ __ um

Write dr words to finish the sentences.

1. Jess has a red __ __ __ __ __.

2. The big __ __ __ __ went
boom! Boom! Boom!

dr

fr

Trace over

fr fr fr fr fr

Copy

fr

Trace over the sounds and write the new words.

fr + og = __________

fr + ost = __________

fr + esh = __________

fr + ill = __________

Trace over the correct fr word.

The green (frod, frog) hopped onto the rock.

Trace over

gr gr gr gr gr gr

Copy

gr

Trace over the gr words in red. Hint! There are six words to be found.

g	r	i	p	g	g
r	g	r	u	b	r
a	g	r	a	n	i
b	g	r	e	e	n

Write gr words in the shapes.

gr

tr

Trace over

tr tr tr tr tr tr

Copy

tr

Make tr words.

trot

Write tr words to match the pictures.

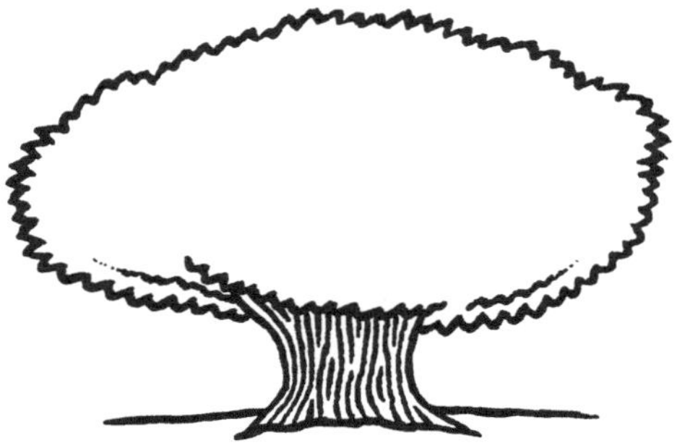

Trace over

ch ch ch ch ch

Copy

ch

Trace over the words that begin with ch in red.

chin slug chill frog

dress chat chop chick

chips

Trace over the sounds and add ch.

bun___ ___

lun___ ___

mun___ ___

ri___ ___

crun___ ___

whi___ ___

ch

sh

Trace over

sh sh sh sh sh sh

Copy

sh

Trace over the sounds and add sh.

Trace over

th th th th th

Copy

th

Trace over the th words. Circle the th sound in red.

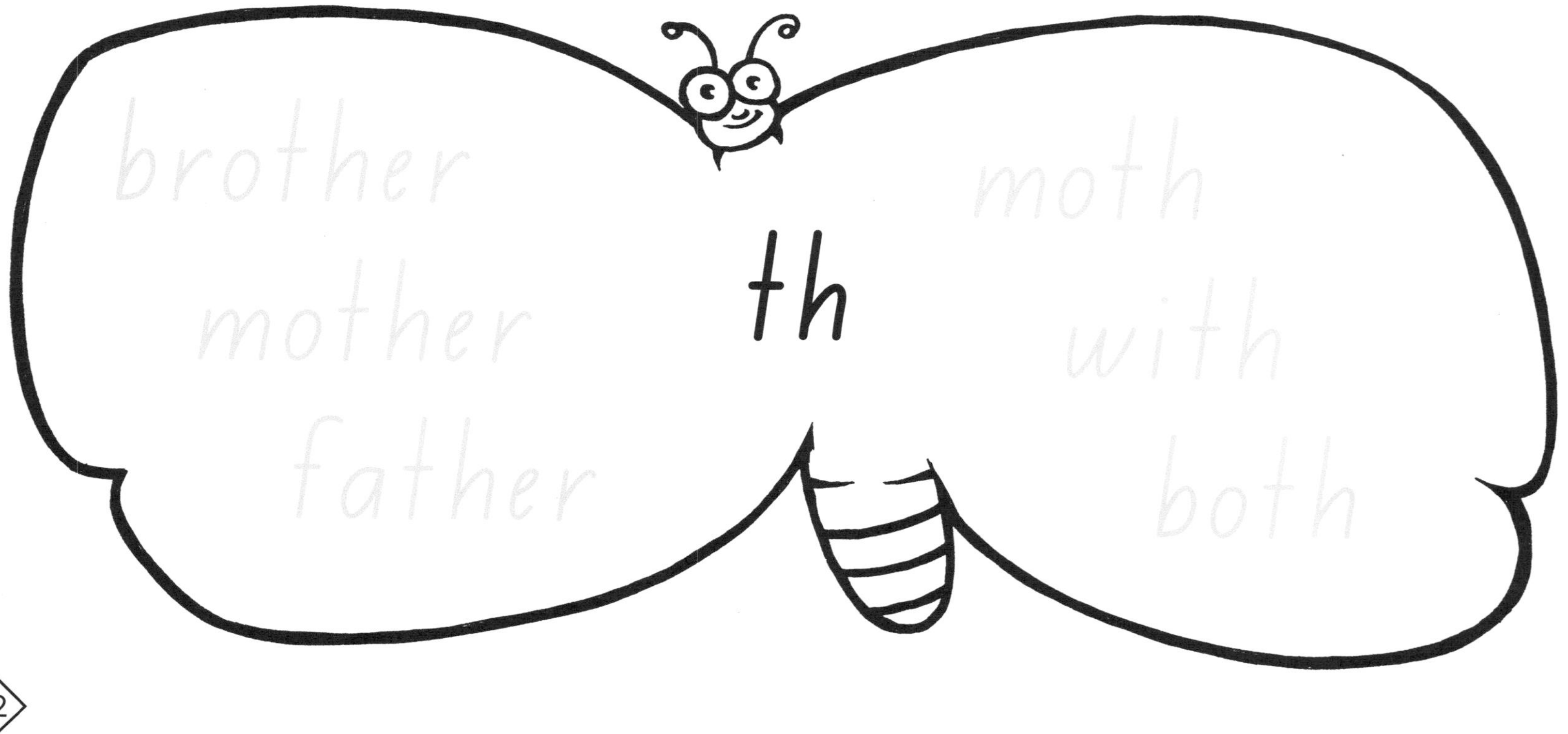

th

wh

Trace over

wh wh wh wh wh

Copy

wh

Trace over the sounds and write the new word.

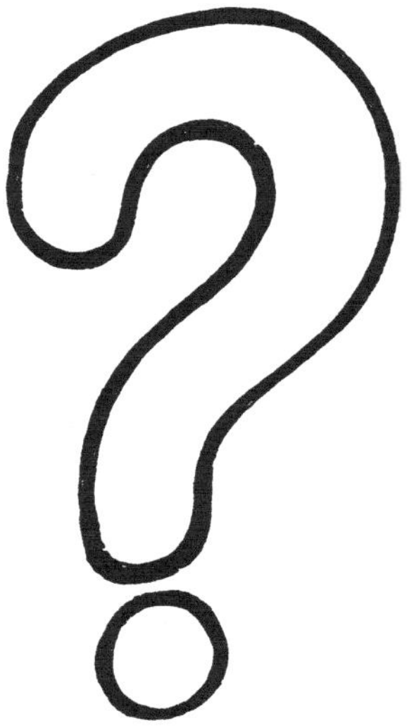

wh + at = ______

wh + en = ______

wh + ip = ______

wh + y = ______

wh + eels = ______

Write wh words in the shapes.

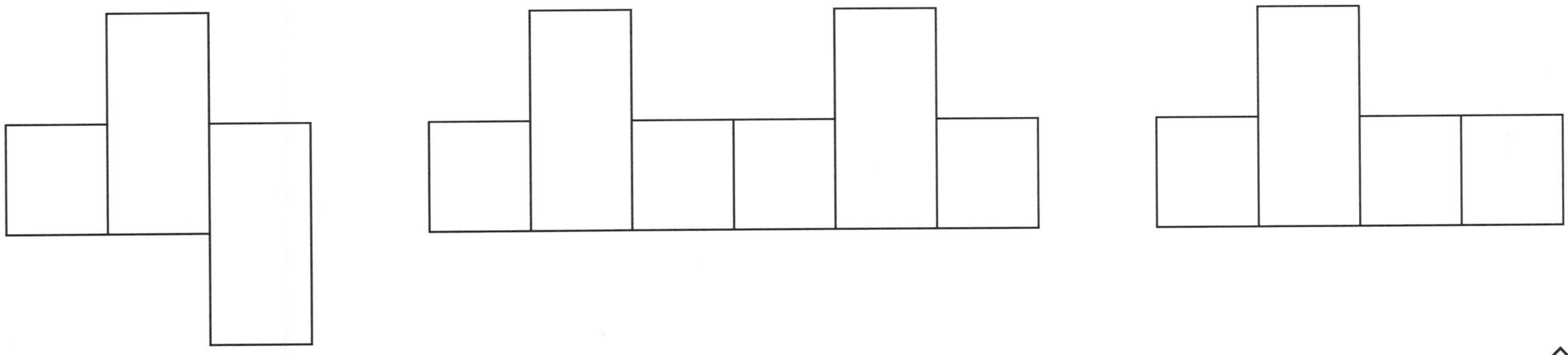

Trace over

ck ck ck ck ck ck

Copy

ck

Trace over the words that end in ck .

Colour the spaces with ck words any colour you like.

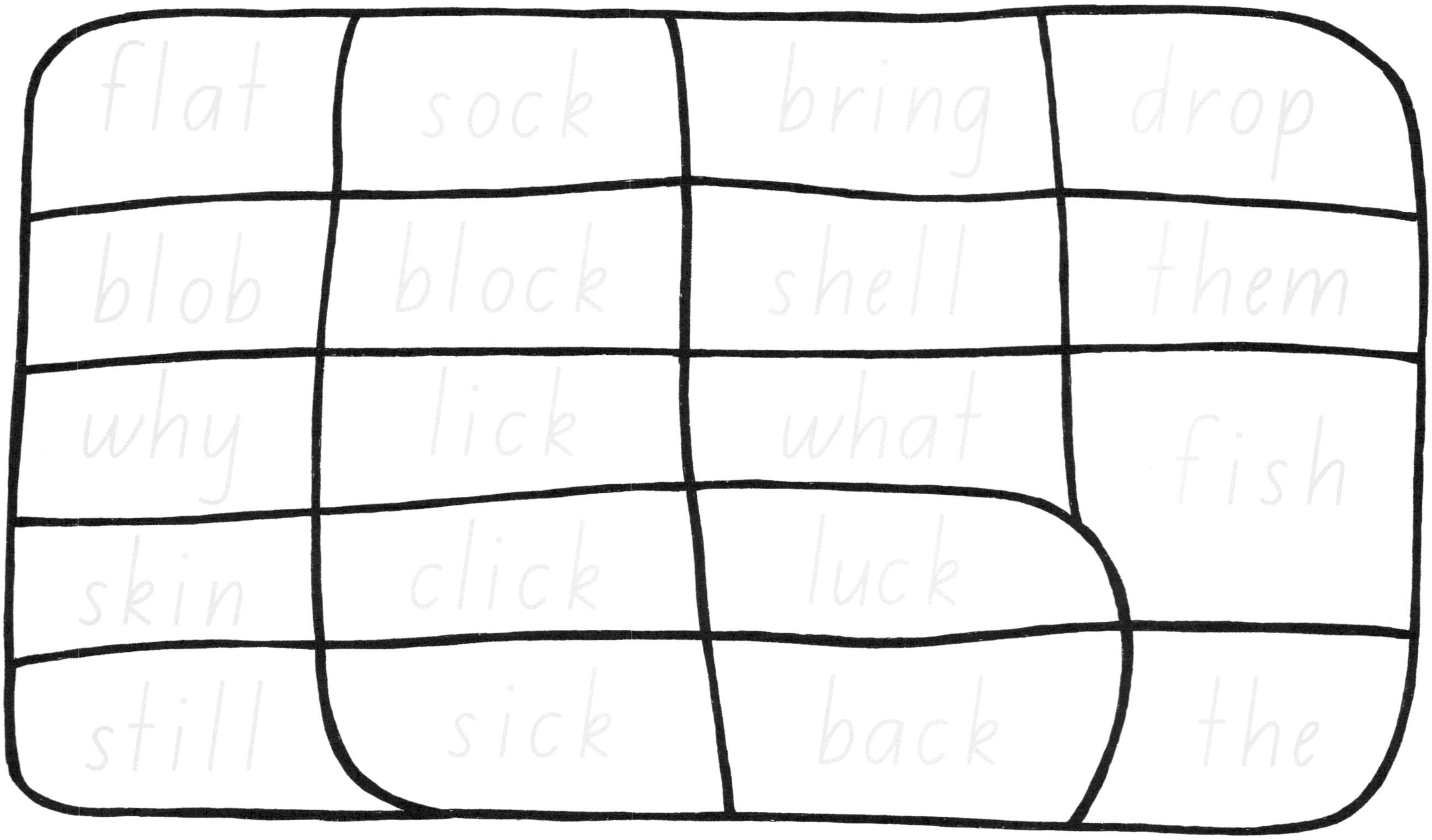

What am I?

I can be any colour. I go over your foot.

I am one of a pair. ___ ___ ___ ___

ck

S S

Trace over

ss ss ss ss ss ss ss

Copy

ss ______________________________

Trace over the sounds and add ss.

ki__ __

cro__ __

le__ __

me__ __

dre__ __

mi__ __

Write ss words to match the pictures.

__ __ __ __ __ __ __ __ __ __ __ __ __

Trace over

ll ll ll ll ll ll

Copy

ll

Make ll words.

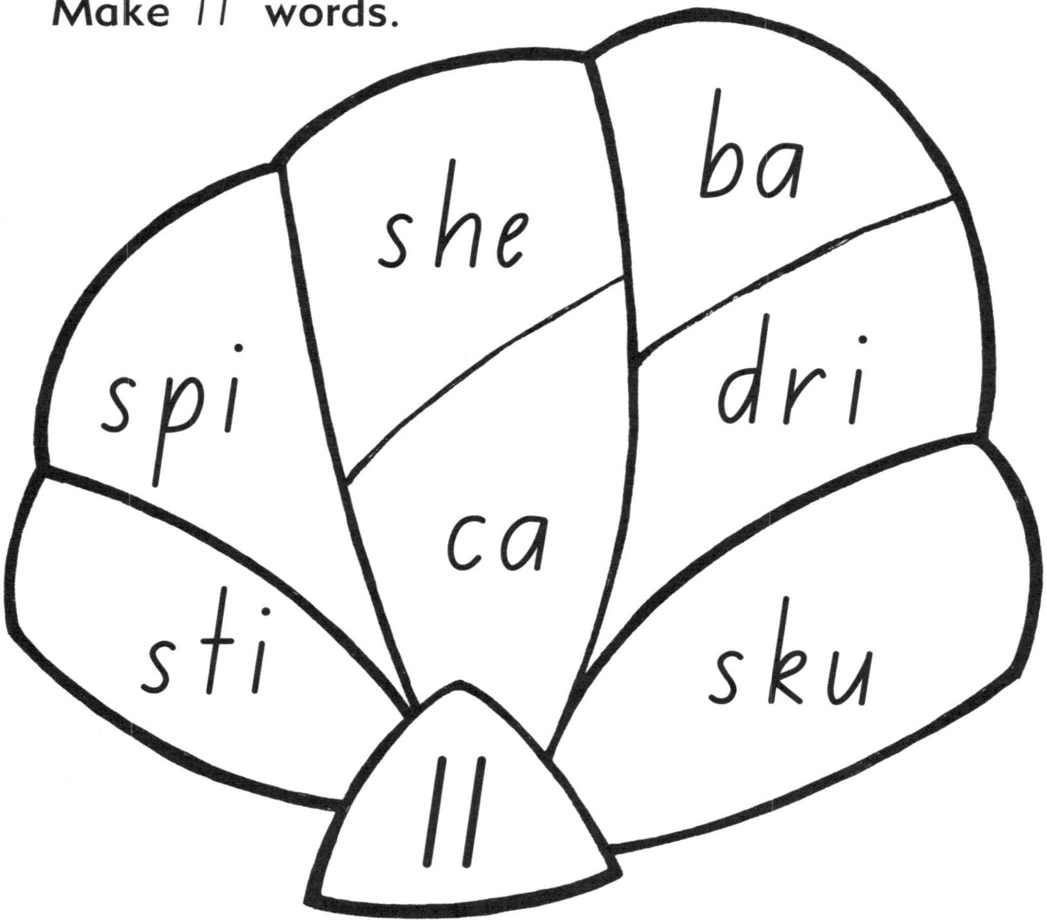

shell

Write two ll words to finish the sentence.

I will throw the _ _ _ _

into the _ _ _ _ grass.

f f

Trace over

ff ff ff ff ff ff

Copy

ff

Trace over the sounds and add ff.

sti___ ___

cu___ ___

cli___ ___

sni___ ___

flu___ ___

pu___ ___

gru___ ___

Write ff words in the shapes.

Trace over

mp mp mp mp mp

Copy

mp

Trace over the mp words. Circle the mp sound in red.

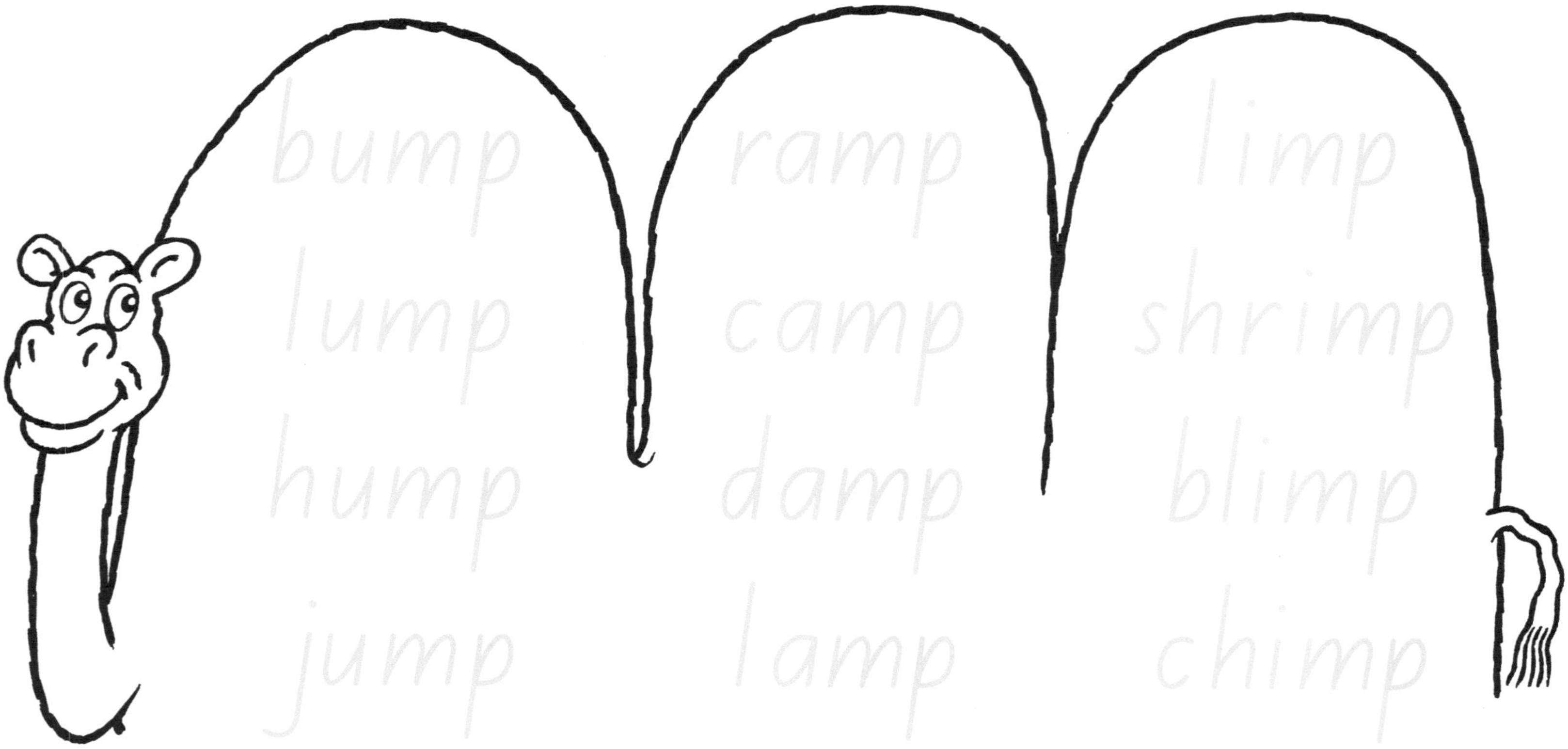

Write mp words to match the pictures.

___ ___ ___ ___ ___ ___ ___ ___ ___ ___ ___ ___ ___

mp

ng

Trace over

ng ng ng ng ng

Copy

ng

Trace over the words that end in ng.

Colour the spaces with ng words any colour you like.

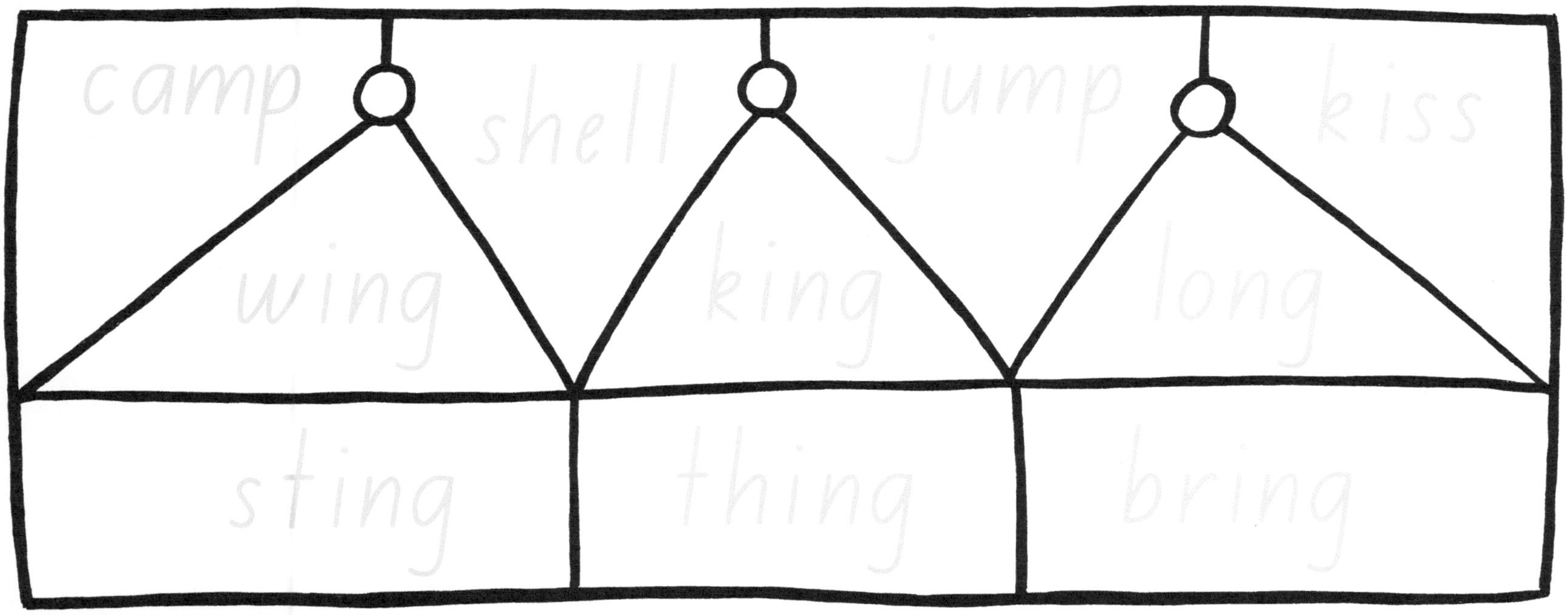

Write rhyming words that end in ng.

wing ______ ______

long ______ ______

rang ______ ______

Trace over

nk nk nk nk nk

Copy

nk

Trace over the sounds and add nk.

ta ___ ___

pi ___ ___

ba ___ ___

sti ___ ___

sa ___ ___

si ___ ___

wi ___ ___

thi ___ ___

Write three nk words to finish the sentence.

I ___ ___ ___ ___ ___ I will wear my ___ ___ ___ ___ hat to the ___ ___ ___ ___.

nk

nt

Trace over

nt nt nt nt nt nt

Copy

nt

Trace over the nt words. Circle the ent words in red.

Write nt words in the shapes.

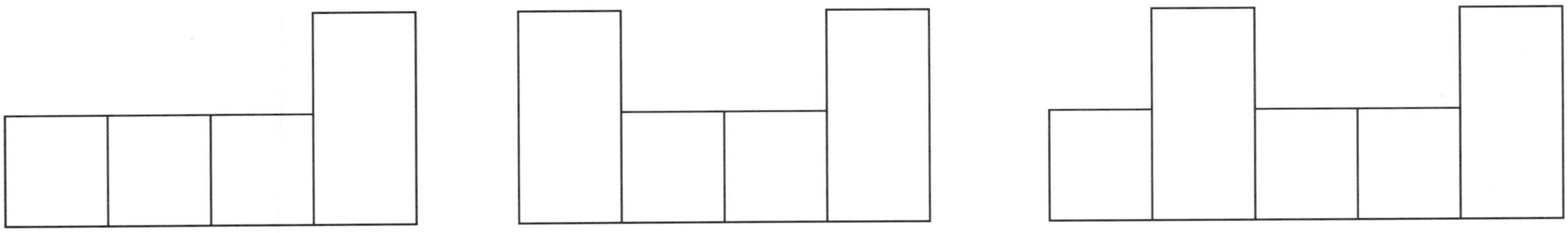

Trace over

nd nd nd nd nd

Copy

nd

Trace over the sounds and add nd.

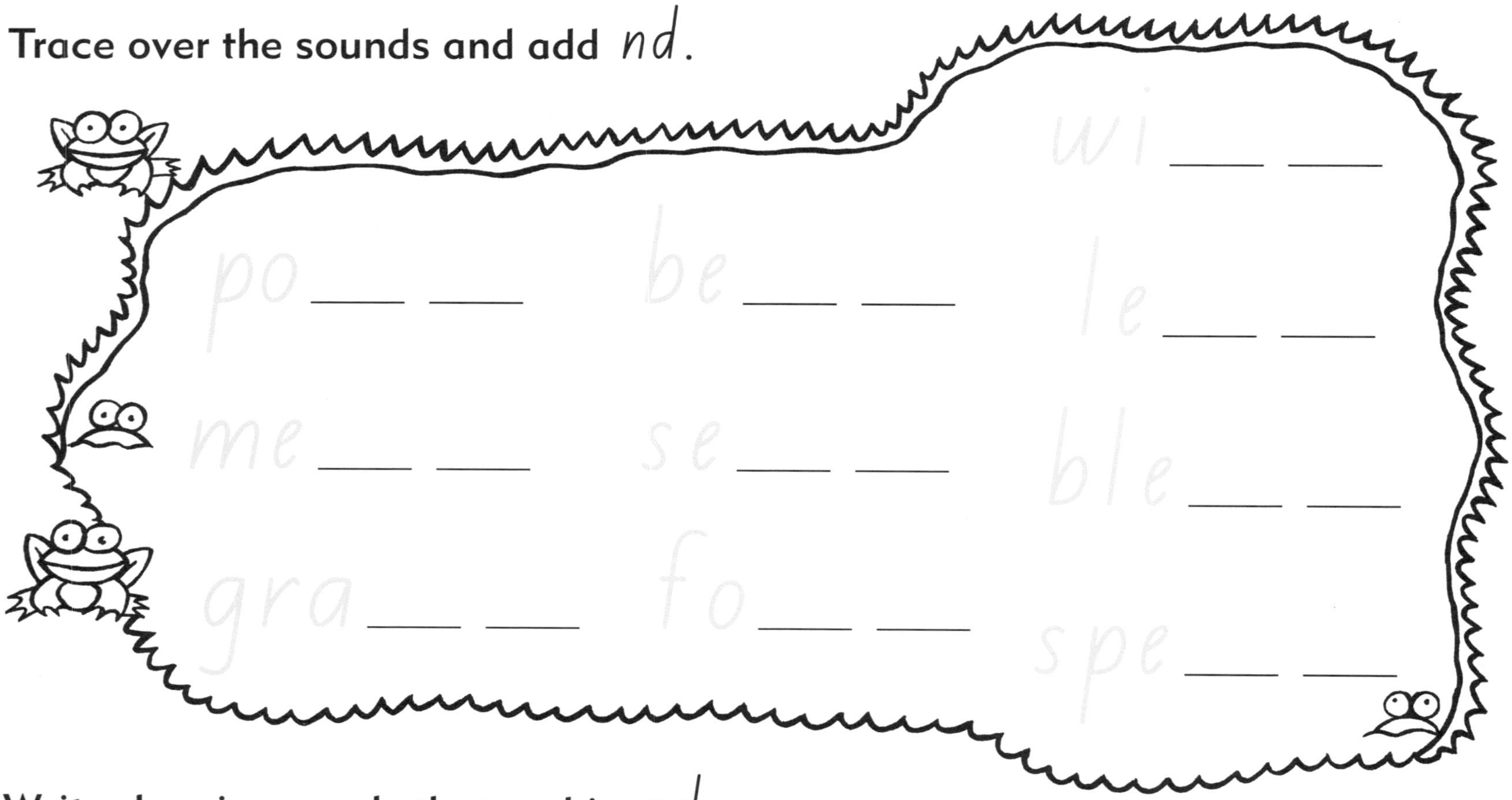

Write rhyming words that end in nd.

send ______________ ______________

______________ ______________

pond ______________

nd

Giant Wordsearch

Find as many words as you can in this giant wordsearch. Remember! Words can be written down, across, on the diagonal and can also be spelt backwards! There are 17 words to find. GOOD LUCK!

f	s	z	d	b	l	t	s
i	k	t	r	l	n	f	l
s	i	l	u	i	y	r	i
h	s	k	m	c	l	i	p
p	s	c	p	o	k	l	m
b	l	a	c	k	t	l	i
s	r	m	l	e	s	s	w
t	z	p	x	k	c	o	s
w	h	y	s	n	i	f	f